D0987106

NOVA ET VETERA:

The Theology of Tradition in American Catholicism

The 1987 Père Marquette
Theology Lecture

NOVA ET VETERA:
The Theology of Tradition in American Catholicism

by

GERALD FOGARTY
Professor of Religious Studies
University of Virginia

MARQUETTE UNIVERSITY PRESS
MILWAUKEE, WISCONSIN 53233

Library of Congress Catalogue Card Number: 87-60584

© Copyright 1987
Marquette University Press

ISBN 0-87462-542-4

Preface

The 1987 Père Marquette Lecture is the eighteenth in a series inaugurated to celebrate the Tercentenary of the missions and explorations of Père Jacques Marquette, S.J. (1637-1675). The Marquette University Theology Department, founded in 1952, launched these annual lectures by distinguished theologians under the title of the Père Marquette Lectures in 1969. The 1987 Lecture is a central event in the year long celebration of Marquette's twenty-five years of experience in graduate theology, the doctoral and master's degree programs, which were the outgrowth of a solidly academic undergraduate structure.

The 1987 lecture was delivered at Marquette University, April 5, 1987, by the Rev. Gerald P. Fogarty, S.J., Professor of Religious Studies at the University of Virginia.

Fr. Fogarty holds a doctorate in history from Yale University and did his theological studies at Woodstock College and Union Theological Seminary in New York.

Fr. Fogarty's own contributions to Church History and Historical Theology include articles in the *Catholic Historical Review,* the *Archivum Historiae Pontificiae,* and the

U.S. Catholic Historian. His books are *The Vatican and the Americanist Crisis: Denis J. O'Connell, American Agent in Rome, 1885-1903* and *The Vatican and the American Hierarchy from 1870 to 1965.* He has just finished a third book on American Catholic biblical scholarship to be published by Harper and Row.

In this lecture Fr. Fogarty attempts to show that the notion of tradition and of its relationship to Sacred Scripture which the Second Vatican Council adopted was the very notion of tradition in the American Church prior to 1870. The concept of tradition that developed after 1870 led to an interpretation of papal and conciliar statements different from that originally intended. Among the examples treated are Church-State relations and the biblical question.

NOVA ET VETERA:
The Theology of Tradition in American Catholicism

When the Second Vatican Council convened in October, 1962, the bishops had before them a schema on the "sources of revelation," Scripture and Tradition. Many may have believed that this was the immutable "doctrine" of the Council of Trent. The progressives, however, argued that there was great significance in the Tridentine decree, which had rejected the formulation that revelation is contained "partim in libris . . . partim in . . . traditionibus," and which had, instead, affirmed that revelation is contained "in libris scriptis et sine scripto traditionibus." They had derived their position from the historical research of J.R. Geiselmann and Hubert Jedin and the theological work of Yves Congar, O.P., and Joseph Ratzinger.[1] The first schema, in other words, raised the question of whether Tradition contained revelation separate from that of Scripture. It was the product of the Theological Commission under the presidency of Cardinal Alfredo Ottaviani, secretary of the Holy Office. As Joseph Ratzinger pointed out, this position of "Roman school theology" had become so ingrained that the defenders of the first schema had blurred the distinction between doctrine and theology.[2]

Americans had perhaps an even more difficult time in accepting the "new" progressive position, for they lacked a sense of history and tended to use the immediate past as the norm for judging the entire past. The "new" position, which would make Scripture and Tradition intimately related, was, in fact, the position expressed by the American Catholic Church in the first half of the nineteenth century. This essay will trace the "old" position up to Vatican I, the loss of that position in the latter part of the nineteenth century, and its re-emergence at Vatican II.

I. Tradition as the Lived Experience of the Church

In 1784, John Carroll, recently named superior of the American mission, was compelled to address the question of the relation between Scripture and Tradition. The occasion was a pamphlet published by Charles Wharton, former chaplain to the Catholic congregation in Worchester, England, who had left the Catholic Church and embraced Anglicanism. To justify his conversion, he argued against certain Catholic doctrines on the grounds that they were not contained in Scripture. Carroll demanded to know by what right Wharton assumed

as a principle, that God communicated nothing more to his church, than is contained in his written word? He knows, that we have always asserted, that the *whole* word of God, unwritten, as well as written, is the christian's rule of faith. It was incumbent then on him, before he discarded this rule, to prove either, that no more was revealed, than is written; or that revealed doctrines derive their claim to our belief, not from God's infallible testimony, but from their being reduced to writing. He has not attempted this; and I will venture to say, he would have attempted it in vain, even with the assistance of his Chillingworth. Happy indeed it is for mankind, that no efforts to this purpose can succeed; for if the catholic rule of faith could be proved unsafe, what security have we for the authenticity, the genuineness, the incorruptibility of Scripture itself: How do we know, but by the tradition that is, by the living doctrine of the catholic church, which are the true and genuine gospels? . . . The testimony therefore of the catholic church, certified in the tradition of all ages, is the ground, upon which we and others admit the divine authority of holy writ.[3]

For Carroll, Scripture and Tradition were not separate sources of revelation, but were closely intertwined because "tradition" was "the living doctrine of the catholic church."

Carroll saw an intimate link between tradition and testimony, on the one hand, and Scripture, on the other, for together they constituted the "word of God." Challenging Wharton, he asked:

And, pray, what is the tradition, to which we recur, but *the word of God* delivered down to us by the testimony of the fathers, and in the public doctrine of the catholic church: Does not the Chaplain himself receive the *written word* of God from the same testimony and tradition? Why is it less to be depended on in witnessing the unwritten word of God, than in delivering down, and separating the true and genuine books of Scripture from those, which are false or corrupted? He demands with St. Cyprian, *whence we have our tradition?* We answer, from the apostles, from their successors, from the attestation of christians spread throughout the world; and St. Augustin proves our right to assign this origin; because, says he, ["]what the universal church holds and was not instituted in a council, but was always maintained, is most reasonably concluded to be derived from apostolical institution.["][4]

For Carroll, then, tradition was a living testimony to the authentic books of Scripture as well as to the interpretation of those books. Not himself an original theologian, he was merely reflecting the theology and apologetics of his age.[5] In 1789, he was elected the first Bishop of Baltimore. As his pastoral obligations increased, he did not, unfortunately, again turn his pen to trying to explain the relationship between Scripture and Tradition. His later concern about the Bible was more on a practical level of providing an American edition of the Douay Bible.

The question of the relationship between Scripture and Tradition again arose in the American Church in the context of the Protestant attacks on Catholics in the 1830s. In 1833, the American bishops assembled for the Second Provincial Council. In their pastoral letter, they continued Carroll's theological orientation. They wrote: "We know not that it is the word of God, except by the testimony of that cloud of holy witnesses which the Saviour vouchsafed to establish as our guide through this desert over which we journey towards our permanent abode."[6] The bishops avoided using the term "tradition," but argued that there was need for testimony not only for what constituted the word of God but also for its correct interpretation. Here, they began to reflect on their own concept of the role that bishops played in tradition, their concept of which was closely associated with their sense of episcopal collegiality. As they put it:

> the recorded testimony of those ancient and vener-
> able witnesses, who in every nation and every age,
> proclaimed in the name of the Catholic Church, and
> with its approbation, the interpretation of the Holy
> Bible, whether they were assembled in their councils
> or dispersed over the surface of the Christian world,
> is an harmonious collection of pure light, which
> sheds upon the inspired page the mild lustre which
> renders it pleasing to the eye, grateful to the under-
> standing, and consoling to the heart. [7]

John England, Bishop of Charleston, wrote the pastoral, but he reflected the theology of Francis P. Kenrick. Kenrick had been a theologian at the First Provincial Council, then coadjutor Bishop of Philadelphia (1830-1842), Bishop of Philadelphia (1842-1851), and Archbishop of Baltimore (1851-1863). Widely regarded as the leading theologian among the bishops, he published the first edition of his *Theologia Dogmatica* in 1839. In his treatise on the Word of God, he tried to provide a norm for the rule of faith. "A full and adequate rule of faith within the Christian economy," he wrote,

> must necessarily be referred to the time of Christ and the Apostles, and then suit the condition of men through all ages; but the Scripture of the New Testament, as a rule of faith, cannot be referred to the age of Christ, nor to the beginning of the apostolic preaching: for it is evident that many years elapsed before anything was consigned to writing. The apostolic writings are not known to have been collected together until the second century; and some were not recognized by some churches for another four centuries. [8]

Kenrick's sources for his treatise were the Fathers, Catholic and Protestant writers in England, and several nineteenth-century German Catholic theologians. Only rarely did he refer to St. Thomas Aquinas or other scholastics. In introducing the notion of "tradition," he strongly recommended Johann Adam Möhler's *Symbolik*. In Kenrick's exposition,

> We have demonstrated that the written word cannot be the basis for a perfect and unique rule of faith; for it needs both a witness and an interpreter. What then is that certain basis which Christ established, in order that men could attain revealed truths? It is, as we have proven, the harmonious preaching of the Apostolic ministry, public and solemn doctrine. Moreover,

> since inspiration and revelation lay claim not to individuals, nor even to the gathering of the Pastors, but is only a type of assistance, by which they can once for all preserve the faith handed down to the saints, therefore the rule which they follow in the very act of teaching is *tradition,* that is the very doctrine of the predecessors, the very faith of the whole Church, derived all the way from the Apostolic age.[9]

Kenrick was not concerned with a sense of "tradition" that meant "some sort of vague rumor preserved in the memory of some people." For him, "*tradition,* which is the rule of our faith, is contained in the greatest part in Scripture, and celebrated back through the ages in the monuments and documents of Christian antiquity, and the customs and public worhsip of the Christian faithful throughout the world."[10] Not only was much of tradition "contained in the Scriptures, which we know to have been written under the divine outpouring," but, if "the basis of tradition is removed, the whole structure of revelation seemed to fall into ruins" and some thinkers were even led to "impugn the inspiration of Scripture."[11]

In explaining inspiration, Kenrick focused primarily on the Church's acceptance of the books as inspired rather than on how inspiration

operated on the writer. Trent, he acknowledged, had stated that all the books and all
the parts of the Old and New Testaments
were to be accepted as holy and canonical, but
there was a wide range of Catholic opinions
about the nature of inspiration.[12] With
debates raging outside the Church on the
meaning of inspiration, Kenrick was confident
that "with the Church as witness and teacher,
Catholics hold the inspiration of Scriptures."
Even those who denied the authority of the
Church were forced to admit that the "certi-
tude of the inspiration of all the books, can
hardly . . . be found without the authority of
the teaching Church."[13] For Kenrick, the
Church was the external argument for the inspiration of Scripture and complemented the
"internal arguments" of prophecies and mira-
cles.[14] Scripture and the living authority of
the Church, then, were inextricably linked to
preserve revelation.

Kenrick did not embrace any particular
theory of inspiration, but he did treat of its
extent. In answering the objection that science
seemed to deny what was contained in Scripture, he argued:

> The Scriptures, by divine counsel, are written down, in order that, learned in the things which pertain to salvation, we might know the works and benefits of God toward men, and the obligations which we ought to assume. About physical things, the sacred writers used the accepted modes of speaking; somewhat popular phrases, borrowed from the appearance of things, were even accustomed to be used by them . . . .[15]

Kenrick anticipated some of the later theories that inspiration did not extend to *obiter dicta* in Scripture. He also asserted that Scripture did not always have to be interpreted literally – a theme related to his concept of tradition that he developed in his translation of the Bible, on which he began work in 1842.

Tradition, for Kenrick, was something living, even prior to the writing of Scripture. His norm for the proper interpretation of Scripture was the consensus of the fathers.[16] Here, of course, he was not original, but the concept shaped his approach to the continuing teaching authority in the Church. The Church of the Apostles and of the Fathers and of his own age continued to be under divine guidance in such a manner that one or even many bishops could fall into error, but "infallibility" or "the privilege of inerrancy" continued to reside "in the body of the bishops, under the presidency of the Roman Pontiff."[17] In short, just as the consensus of the Fathers was the norm for the interpretation of Scripture, the consensus of the bishops, in unity with the pope, was the norm for the teaching of the Church.

Kenrick later took an analogous approach to accepting scientific data, which seemed to contradict the Scripture. In 1860, he published his version of the Pentateuch. He was principally concerned with the argument of geologists that the earth was considerably older than the Genesis account would imply. "We feel bound to respect the judgment of the learned," he wrote, "when they agree so decidedly in declaring the results of their investigations." When the learned disagreed, however, they would "detract much from the weight which they might otherwise have, and our veneration for the sacred text does not allow us hastily to abandon its letter, or absolutely to embrace what does not appear to harmonize with it."[18] In other words, Kenrick would follow the consensus of "the learned" in abandoning the literal interpretation of Scripture. But here he thought he had an important precedent in Catholic tradition.

Kenrick reminded his readers that the Fathers were not in agreement in interpreting the Genesis account literally. That "diversity of views" among the Fathers, he stated, "shows that on this point the tradition of the Church was not absolute and dogmatical, so that if, with the progress of science, it become manifest, that a vast succession of ages can alone account for the structure of the earth . . . such indefinite periods may be admitted, without departing in any respect from the authoritative teachings of antiquity." In regard to the historicity of the Genesis account, he insisted that all that had been "divinely revealed" in Genesis was "the origin of all things from the creative act of God, and the creation of man, as stated by the inspired author."[19]

Kenrick's theological method enabled him to see tradition as something dynamic and living and to be open to new discoveries. Unfortunately, that method was soon to be eclipsed by developments in Europe.

II. Vatican I and Tradition as a Deposit

By the middle of the nineteenth century, the European Church was in a state of siege, politically and intellectually. To combat the new trend of rationalism, the Holy See came to rely increasingly on neo-Thomism, which was in fact not so much a return to Thomas Aquinas, but to a school of Thomism, which placed truth, not in the act of judgment, but in the formation of a concept.[20] Pius IX, who had opened his pontificate as an apparent liberal, epitomized the reaction of the Church against the new movements. Increasingly, he spoke in absolutes. Moreover, his concept of tradition centered on the papal office. "La Tradizione son'io," was his unfortunate formulation.[21] The crowning achievements of his orientation were the "Syllabus of Errors," as will be seen, and the First Vatican Council. The theological interpretations produced by these two events would create a new understanding of the meaning of tradition.

Kenrick had emphasized tradition as the process of preserving the correct interpretation of Scripture. The council now declared

that "all those things are to be believed with
divine and Catholic faith which are contained
in the word of God, written or handed down,
and which the Church, either by a solemn
judgment, or by her ordinary and universal
magisterium, proposes for belief as having
been divinely revealed."[22] "The doctrine of
faith," the council continued, "is like a divine
deposit handed down to the Spouse of Christ,"
the Church.[23] The formulation was due to
Johannes Baptist Franzelin, S.J., professor
of dogmatic theology at the Gregorian University. It focused on tradition as content and
came dangerously close to equating it with the
content of pronouncements of the magisterium, particularly the papal magisterium.
Moreover, the Council of Trent had referred
to the "Gospel" of Christ as "the source of all
salutary truth and of moral discipline," which
were "contained in Scripture and in unwritten
traditions."[24] In quoting Trent, Vatican I
truncated the text. Instead of truth and moral
discipline, "revelation" was now said to be contained in Scripture and unwritten traditions.[25]
As Congar has noted, this truncation "sug-
gests the idea of two parallel and partial
sources."[26]

Franzelin's concept of tradition would gradually come to dominate theological discussion for the next seventy-five years. The form of Thomism he represented was further reinforced in 1879, when Leo XIII issued *Aeterni Patris*, calling for the Thomistic revival. The neo-Thomism that the encyclical promoted, however, was a-historical. It emphasized the objective universality of truth. In the words of Gerald McCool, "it was an impersonal science whose strength lay in its Aristotelian conceptual form, logical techniques, and metaphysical principles. One of the most important sources of its power was its respect for the objective truth of revelation and for the public and authoritative teaching of the universal Church."[27] One of its significant weaknesses, McCool continued, was that "it was unaffected by the personality and the cultural milieu of individual thinkers. Differences in time, historical outlook, and cultural expression were accidental."[28] In the hands of later theologians, there was a tendency to analyze words rather than concepts and to seek in St. Thomas the answers to contemporary problems rather than to use his method to solve them.

Franzelin had been named a cardinal by Pius IX in 1876. In 1879, Leo XIII summoned Camillo Mazzella, S.J., first dean of Woodstock College in Maryland, to take up Franzelin's post in dogmatic theology at the Roman College. At Franzelin's death in 1886, Mazzella was elevated to the sacred college. His place at the Roman College was taken by Louis Billot, S.J. Each would develop Franzelin's concept of tradition and significantly alter the understanding of Catholic doctrine in several areas. Two examples will suffice to illustrate this change particularly in relation to the American Church: Church-State relations and biblical scholarship. Both questions came to the fore at the end of the century. Both became subjected to the new understanding of tradition, but in different ways. Both were intertwined not only by occurring at the same time but also on the grounds for theological opposition to each of them.

A. CHURCH-STATE RELATIONS
AND RELIGIOUS LIBERTY

Since the founding of Maryland in 1634, American Catholics had not only accepted but also developed a positive position in favor of religious liberty, achieved through the separation of Church and State.[29] In 1837, the American bishops sharply distinguished between the "civil and political allegiance" that citizens owed to the states and the federal government and the "spiritual and ecclesiastical" loyalty that Catholics rendered to the pope. None of the states, they declared, "claims any supremacy or domination over us in our spiritual or ecclesiastical concerns: nor does it claim any such right or power over any of our fellow citizens, of whatsoever religion they may be: and if such claim was made, neither would our fellow citizens, nor would we submit thereto."[30] The Americans did not feel bound by Gregory XVI's *Mirari Vos* condemning Lamennais' espousal of freedom of conscience for everyone and of the separation of Church and State.[31] A few years earlier, the Belgian bishops had also decided quietly not to promulgate the encyclical on the grounds that it did not apply to them.[32] Encyclicals were not yet seen as containing a universal and immutable interpretation of tradition. Such a mentality continued even in regard to Pius IX's "Syllabus of Errors" in 1864.

The syllabus included among its condemned errors: "that the church should be separated from the state and the state from the church";[33] and "in our age it is no longer expedient that the Catholic religion be held as the only religion of the state, with all other cults whatsoever being excluded."[34] Here seemed to be a clear condemnation of the pastoral of the American bishops in 1837. Archbishop John McCloskey of New York, who would become the nation's first cardinal eleven years later, expressed his concern to Archbishop Martin John Spalding of Baltimore. "It can hardly be doubted," he wrote, that the syllabus

> places us in a state of *apparent* antagonism, as far at least as our principles are concerned, to the institutions under which we live – and affords a grand pretext to the fanatics who are eager to get up a crusade against us. God knows best what is for the good of His Church.[35]

The most influential, and subsequently misunderstood, interpretation of the Syllabus came from Bishop Félix Dupanloup of Orléans. Following the lead of an article by Carlo Maria Curci, S.J., in *Civiltà cattolica* the previous year, Dupanloup applied to the Syllabus the distinction between "thesis" or ideal and "hypothesis." In his analysis, what Pius IX condemned were absolute theses, from which there could never be any deviation. Hence, the pope condemned as an absolute the proposition that the Church should be separated from the State with the result that religious indifferentism would become the norm. In Dupanloup's presentation, the Catholic "thesis" was harmony between Church and State, which could be achieved by a variety of "hypotheses," one of which was a union between the two. Pius IX thanked Dupanloup, particularly for his castigation of the radicals who had made the syllabus necessary. Significantly, however, the pope did not repudiate Dupanloup's thesis-hypothesis interpretation. [36]

For the moment, Dupanloup's distinction had assuaged the fears of some of the American bishops. Archbishop Spalding used the distinction in a pastoral letter to his people:

> To stretch the words of the Pontiff, evidently intended for the standpoint of European radicals and infidels, so as to make them include the state of things established in this country by our Constitution in regard to liberty of conscience, of worship, and of the press, were [sic] manifestly unfair and unjust. [37]

But Spalding and Dupanloup were writing in 1864. Over the next thirty years, the new theology became ingrained and the nuances given to the interpretation of papal utterances were lost. In later theology, Dupanloup's distinction was misconstrued to mean that the Catholic "thesis" was the union of Church and State and the "hypothesis" was what was merely tolerable as long as the Church had its freedom. In time, a theological misinterpretation became synonymous with official doctrine.

The battle over Americanism in the 1890s indicated just how much the new concept of tradition had been taken over in Rome. The hierarchy in the United States was sharply divided over the issue of Americanizing the Church. Archbishop John Ireland of St. Paul and Cardinal James Gibbons of Baltimore wanted to show the compatibility of Catholicism with American culture. They praised the freedom given to the Church by the American separation of Church and State. Their opponents, led by Archbishop Michael Corrigan of New York, challenged this Americanizing program. In 1895, Leo XIII issued his apostolic letter, *Longinqua Oceani,* to the

American Church. In it, he warned that "it would be very erroneous to draw the conclusion that in America is to be sought the type of the most desirable status of the Church, or that it would be universally lawful or expedient for the State and Church to be, as in America, dissevered and divorced." While Leo did not condemn the American separation of Church and State, he did declare that the American Church "would bring forth more abundant fruits if, in addition to liberty, she enjoyed the favor of the laws and the patronage of the public authority."[38] The issue of whether the American separation of Church and State should be universally applied became more controversial within a few years.

In 1897, Walter Elliott's *Life of Father Hecker* was translated into French. Isaac Hecker, who had founded the Paulists, a congregation of priests without religious vows, was not trained in Thomistic theology. He thus used terms, such as "active and passive virtues," which were subject to misinterpretation in a Thomistic context. In France, he was transformed into the priest of the future. "Americanism" had become an international issue.

In August, 1897, Fribourg, Switzerland, hosted the fourth – and last – International Catholic Scientific Congress. The papers presented illustrated all the new orientations in theology. M.-J. Lagrange, O.P., as will be seen below, gave his first paper on the historical criticism of the Pentateuch. From the United States came two speakers. Father John Zahm, C.S.C., of the University of Notre Dame, spoke on evolution and dogma, a topic on which he was then completing a book. Monsignor Denis J. O'Connell, former rector of the American College in Rome, took up the controversial subject of Church-State relations and religious liberty in a paper entitled "A New Idea in the Life of Father Hecker."

O'Connell began by praising the American constitutional system, which was based on the British and American Common Law. The philosophical underpinnings of the Common Law, he continued, were expressed in the Declaration of Independence, which stated that "all men are created equal and are endowed by their Creator with certain inalienable rights." This system he contrasted with the Roman Law, according to which individuals had only the rights that the state gave them.

The Common Law, he continued, meant that no individual, no matter what office he held, was above the law. Such a system, he concluded was more compatible with the Catholic doctrine of the dignity conferred on the individual in Baptism than the Roman Law, which was pagan in origin. Within the framework of the advantages of the Common Law, O'Connell then turned to the question of Church and State. The First Amendment to the Constitution, he asserted, guaranteed that the Church could conduct her affairs free from any governmental interference. In his development of this theme, however, he displayed the misinterpretation of the thesis-hypothesis reasoning since its introduction by Dupanloup. "However beautiful and true in theory," he said, "may be the doctrine of the legal union of Church and State, in practice it has unfortunately been found but too often to work to the grave injury of the Church by diminishing her liberty, and giving to laymen sometimes possessed of little piety, the pretext for interfering in the administration of her affairs." He concluded that the American "hypothesis" seemed "to work as well as any other actual system we are acquainted with."[39]

Nothing could have been a more inept use of Dupanloup's original distinction, but it was the one then generally accepted.

The period after the Fribourg congress witnessed a rising crescendo of attacks on Americanism. From March 3 to April 9, 1898, a series of articles appeared in *La Vérité,* entitled "L'Americanisme Mystique" and signed "Martel." The author was Father Charles Maignen of the Society of the Brothers of St. Vincent de Paul. He explicitly attacked O'Connell's argumentation. He asserted that, in theory, "the State, like the individual, has the duty to profess the Christian faith; but, in practice, *Americanism* speaks and acts as if *the thesis* ought everywhere to give way to *the hypothesis.*" "The hypothesis," he continued, was "limited, in its application, by two pontifical decisions, and there is no right to allow their doctrine to pass out of date." Here Maignen cited condemned propositions of the "Syllabus of Errors," which, he contended, "contain nothing more than the doctrine of *Americanism* . . . But, they are *reproved, proscribed* and *condemned* by the authority of the Holy See, which *wishes* and *orders* all the children of the Catholic Church to hold them as *reproved, proscribed* and *condemned.*"[40] Maignen, like O'Connell, had totally misconstrued Dupanloup's use of "thesis" and "hypothesis."

Maignen saved much of his venom for Hecker, who, he asserted, had so emphasized the interior guidance of the Holy Spirit that he denigrated the external authority of the Church. The Paulist, furthermore, had praised "active virtues," appropriate for republicans, over "passive virtues," more suited for monarchists. The American, Maignen declared, had also watered down doctrine in order to gain converts and had relegated religious vows to the middle ages. Hecker's pernicious influence could be seen in the thought of his followers, especially Cardinal Gibbons, Archbishop Ireland, Archbishiop John Keane, former rector of the Catholic University, and O'Connell.[41] Maignen's attacks were scurrilous, but he seemed to gain official approval. He gathered his articles together as a book and had it published in Rome with the *imprimatur* of Alberto Lepidi, O.P., the Master of the Sacred Palace.

During the summer of 1898, Leo XIII appointed a commission, under the presidency of Cardinal Mazzella, to investigate Americanism. At the same time, the question of biblical criticism and evolution also fell under Roman scrutiny. O'Connell described the situation for Ireland:

> A perfect feeling of spite & madness is running wild here just now. They are really acting & talking like men that have lost their senses. The poor pope is trying to find a cool place to sit down in and care for his health, and the others, like powers long kept confined, are now rushing like [illegible] lions for their prey, before the Pope dies. It is the pent up madness of 10 years that is breaking out. This is their "hour." Another party of them is engaged in preparing a decree against Evolution, soon to appear, and some wanted a condemnation of "La Revue Biblique." Rev. Dr. [Salvatore] Minocchi, a prominent Hebrew scholar at Florence and translator of many of the books from the Hebrew, received one morning without any intimation or explanation an order to write nothing more on Scripture. [Giovanni] Genocchi is trying to arrange his case.

He concluded his description of this flurry of activity by noting that Louis Duchesne, the French Church historian, "says he always observed that the H. Office is worse during the months of June & July."[42] At the same time, O'Connell's friend, Gennochi, an Italian exegete, reported that some people in Rome were beginning to consider "critico-biblical studies as an apparent part of dangerous Americanism."[43]

The references which O'Connell had made to the *Revue Biblique* concerned Lagrange's denunciation in Rome by Archbishop Piavi, O.F.M., Latin Patriarch of Jerusalem. The Franciscan had accused Lagrange the previous April of embracing "German rationalism" in the address he had given in Fribourg and which had been published in the *Revue*. Though Lagrange's superiors supported him, they did, shortly thereafter, recommend that he publish a proposed commentary on Genesis in a series of articles, rather than in a book.[44] Biblical scholarship and Americanism at least had in common that they were both under investigation at the same time by the same people. The threads of several different intellectual movements were now being woven together by the conservative theologians.

On January 22, 1899, Leo XIII issued his apostolic letter *Testem Benevolentiae*. The letter condemned the notion "that, in order to bring over to Catholic doctrine those who dissent from it, the Church ought to adapt herself somewhat to our advanced civilization, and, relaxing her ancient rigor, show some indulgence to modern popular theories and methods." The pope was concerned that this notion was applied "not only with regard to the rule of life, but also to the doctrines in which the *deposit of faith* is contained." Advocates of this approach would attempt "to pass over certain heads of doctrines, as if of lesser moment, or to so soften them that they may not have the same meaning which the Church has invariably held."[45]

Leo then questioned some of Hecker's supposed teaching, namely on the role of the Holy Spirit within the individual Christian's life. He condemned those who held that "all external guidance is rejected as superfluous, nay even as somewhat of a disadvantage." This was a caricature of Hecker's theory, but it was clear that the pope feared the theory would jeopardize the role of the Church as the guarantor of the Holy Spirit. On the one hand, he reproached those who seemed to imply that previous ages had "received a lesser outpouring of the Holy Spirit." On the other hand, he asserted that "no one doubts that the Holy Ghost, by His secret incoming into the souls of the just, influences and arouses them by admonition and impulse." Here the pope quoted the Second

Council of Orange which stated that "if any one positively affirms that he can consent to the saving preaching of the Gospel without the illumination of the Holy Ghost, who imparts sweetness to all to consent to and accept the truth, he is misled by a heretical spirit."[46]

The citation of the Second Council of Orange served as a warning to the Americanists that they were suspected of Pelagianism. In case they missed the point, the pope immediately went on to challenge their praise of "natural virtues." It was "hard to see," said Leo, "if we do away with all external guidance . . . , what purpose the more abundant influence of the Holy Ghost, which they make so much of, is to serve." Those who spoke of this abundance of the Spirit seemed also to "extol beyond measure the natural virtues as more in accordance with the ways and requirements of the present day, and consider it an advantage to be richly endowed with them, because they make a man more ready and more strenuous in action." This seemed to imply that "nature . . . , with grace added to it," was "weaker than when left to its own strength." "Rare," indeed, was "the man who really possesses the habit of these natural virtues." Only with "some divine help" could one observe "the whole natural law." "If we do not wish to lose sight of the eternal blessedness to which God in His goodness has destined us," Leo concluded, "of what use are the natural virtues unless the gift and strength of divine grace be added?"[47]

The responses to the apostolic letter reflected the divisions within the hierarchy, both American and European. Archbishop Ireland and Cardinal Gibbons emphatically denied that any American held the condemned positions. Archbishop Corrigan and Archbishop Frederick Katzer of Milwaukee both thanked the pope for exorcising the heresy from the American Church through his infallible authority. The bishops of the provinces of Turin and Vercelli in northern Italy also linked the letter to papal infallibility.[48] In their responses, the conservatives had, therefore, elevated an apostolic letter, addressed to a local church, to the level of an infallible statement. In regard to the Church-State question and religious liberty in the twentieth century, these papal proclamations would be seen as part of the "tradition," which the Church had to defend.

But there was another dimension of *Tes-*

tem Benevolentiae, which linked it to historical criticism of the Bible. Shaped by the battle against rationalism, the letter reflected a low opinion of human nature without grace. Grace became rare and, with the external guidance of the Church, was necessary for human nature to attain its end. This had a direct relationship to the biblical question. According to the prevailing theology, the new exegetes could not apply mere natural criticism to the sacred books, for this would imply that Scripture was a natural work. To preserve the inspiration of Scripture, the exegete had to acknowledge that the mind of the human author was supernaturally elevated to such an extent that his work could not be subjected to comparisons with other ancient near-eastern literature or to any other form of higher criticism, for Scripture had God as its Author. Inspiration had to be restricted to an author, whose name was known by tradition. To accept the possibility that the books of Scripture went through a series of redactions or to argue that several sources were put together to form a given book could mean that inspiration, like grace for the Americanists, would not be rare.

At first blush, Americanism and biblical criticism seemed to have little in common. Only a few progressive thinkers, like O'Connell and Genocchi sensed any connection. Yet, the reactions against both movements ran parallel to one another. In November, 1898, as the Americanists awaited the decision of Leo's commission, Lucien Méchineau, S.J., professor of Scripture at the Gregorian University, published an article accusing Lagrange of going over "to the camp of our adversaries,"[49] Later that month, Leo issued a letter to the Minister General of the Franciscans, warning them of the dangers of some modern tendencies in the study of Scripture. Lagrange was certain that the pope had actually intended the letter for the Dominicans, as a result of the protests of Archbishop Piavi.[50] Finally, on January 28, within a week of *Testem Benevolentiae,* Father Frühwirth, O.P., the Master General, wrote Lagrange, warning him of the letter addressed to the Franciscans. He also ordered that every article to be published in the *Revue biblique* be first submitted to Rome to be read by censors, whom he himself would choose.[51] At least in terms of coincidence in time, there was a relation between Americanism and the biblical question. There was a further relation in the way in which each fell victim to the new theology of tradition.

B. THE BIBLICAL QUESTION

The biblical question, as it developed in the nineteenth century, was focused on the question of inspiration. The theology of inspiration developed to combat the challenge of the rationalists was largely derived from an analysis of St. Thomas' treatment of prophecy.[52] It was again Franzelin who developed the theory, which became dominant. Simply put, Franzelin started with the principle that God is the author of Scripture. He then applied to the notion of "author" all the attributes of a human author.[53] Franzelin's theory, especially in the hands of lesser theologians, left little room for any analysis of the human author, but its influence was obvious on Vatican I's formulation of the nature of inspiration. The Church, said the council, accepted the books to be "sacred and canonical, not because they were carefully composed by human industry alone and were subsequently approved by her authority; nor merely because they contain revelation without error but because, having been written under the inspiration of the Holy Spirit, they have God as their author and as such have been handed down to the Church herself."[54]

In 1893, Leo XIII incorporated Franzelin's theory into his encyclical *Providentissimus Deus*. In regard to apparent contradictions between the Scripture and science, Leo noted, Thomas Aquinas had said that the sacred writers "went by what sensibly appeared."[55] Immediately after treating the natural sciences, the pope declared that "the principles here laid down will apply to cognate sciences, and especially to history."[56] It was but a logical conclusion for the liberal exegetes to develop what they termed "historical appearances." But here they would run into problems.

It was Leo's treatment of inerrancy and inspiration, however, which showed the greatest influence of Franzelin and caused future controversy. Since God is the Author of Scripture, said the pope, inspiration and error were incompatible, "for all the books which the Church receives as sacred and canonical are written wholly and entirely, with all their parts, at the dictation of the Holy Spirit; and so far is it from being possible that any error can coexist with inspiration, that inspiration not only is essentially incompatible with error, but excludes and rejects it as absolutely and necessarily as it is impossible that God Himself, the supreme Truth, can utter that which is not true."[57] As proof, Leo quoted Vatican I in uttering that "God is the author of Scripture," and concluded that the human authors, as instruments, had been so elevated by "supernatural power" that they wrote with "infallible truth." To say otherwise, said the pontiff, would deny that God "was the Author of the entire Scripture."[58] Cardinal Mazzella had drafted that part of the encylical, which so reflected Franzelin's theory.[59]

Two strands of thought now became intertwined. First, the theology of inspiration moved away from its association with the acceptance of the books of the Church and toward identification with authorship. Second, this view was re-enforced by an interpretation of tradition as expressed by the magisterium. In 1890, Fulcran Vigouroux, S.S., treated this theme in his five-volume work, *Les livres saints et la critique rationaliste.* "The Christian tradition," he wrote, "has

always unanimously attributed the composition of the Pentateuch to Moses." Citing the
"Fathers, the doctors, the interpreters and
the Catholic commentators," who had never
deviated from this tradition, he added: "and
the Council of Trent has been a faithful echo
of the belief of the Church in naming Moses
as the author of the first five books of the
Bible, in the Canon of Scriptures." For
Vigouroux, the tradition of the Church, which
Trent had reinforced, could not have been
otherwise, for "the Church itself has received
this belief from the synagogue. It is in effect
certain that, in the era of Our Savior, the
Jews attributed the Pentateuch to Moses." As
proof, Vigouroux had only to cite the six passages where Christ spoke of Moses.[60] In
short, to deny the Mosaic authorship of the
Pentateuch would be to impugn not only the
"tradition" of the Church, as expressed by the
Council of Trent, but also the words of Christ
Himself. Put in other terms, conciliar statements, like Scripture, were first to be interpreted literally. Vigouroux had read back into
Trent the nineteenth-century question of authorship. Not everyone, however, agreed with
his interpretation of the Council of Trent.

M.-J. Lagrange, O.P., had returned to the Fathers to develop his theory of inspiration and tradition. Unwisely perhaps, he concluded that defenders of the Church "will feel more comfortable in the large edifices of traditional theology than in the modern halls, hastily built up, as a provisional refuge by Cardinal Franzelin."[61] As was seen, Lagrange had presented his first paper on historical criticism of the Pentateuch at the same International Catholic Scientific Congress in 1897 where Denis O'Connell spoke on religious liberty. Baron Friedrich von Hügel condensed the paper and translated it into English for publication in the *The Catholic University Bulletin*. Lagrange treated the "tradition" that Moses was the author of the Pentateuch. Here Lagrange drew a distinction: "we get, first, a double modality: Moses is the legislator of Israel, Mosaism is at the bottom of the whole history of the people of God – there is the *historical* tradition; Moses was the redactor of the Pentateuch which we possess; there is the *literary* tradition." Those who defended the Mosaic authorship had failed to make this distinction. There was, moreover, no way to "find a witness to the literary fact of the total

composition." Lagrange illustrated his point
by analogy with the Lord's Prayer. "We generally admit," he wrote,

> that the words of Our Lord have been in a certain
> measure, transformed by the primitive oral teaching
> of the Church; we have in the Gospels two forms of
> the *Pater Noster,* and do not hold ourselves bound
> to maintain that Jesus Christ pronounced them both;
> why then should we believe that Moses wrote both
> forms of the Decalogue?[62]

In this context, Lagrange addressed the
question of whether the Mosaic authorship of
the Pentateuch was part of formal tradition
as a locus of revelation. "Whilst pronouncing
on Canonicity," he wrote, the Council of Trent
had "avoided deciding the question of Authorship." He argued that the council's reference
to the "Pentateuch of Moses" was a "disci-
plinary rule," which "cannot be extended
beyond what is practiced with regard to the
Epistle to the Hebrews, the origin of which
was actually discussed in the council." He
granted that he was asking "something more
for the Pentateuch, yet this will ever remain
the Pentateuch of Moses, if that great man
laid the foundations of its legislation."[63]
Lagrange's interpretation of the binding force

of the Tridentine statement clearly differed from that of Vigouroux.

In the United States, nascent American scholarship was already picking up the new exegesis. In 1891, John B. Hogan, S.S., president of the Divinity College at the Catholic University, began to publish a series of articles in the *American Ecclesiastical Review* on "Clerical Studies." Named president of St. John's Seminary in Brighton, Massachusetts in 1894, Hogan continued the series and published it in book form in 1898. He proposed that seminary education be historically based and lamented that since the middle ages the Bible had "ceased to be at the centre of clerical studies, and this was the direct result of the new movement which gave birth to scholastic theology." The Bible, he continued, was replaced with "logical argument" and "it gradually gave way to the *Sentences* and to Aristotle."[64] While couching his exposition in a simple narration of facts, Hogan was, of course, attacking the scholasticism which Leo had sought to revive.

Hogan was daring in his criterion for the interpretation of Scripture. The literal interpretation, he said, led to defensiveness against

the new sciences of astronomy, geology, and
evolution. Those who adhered to this interpretation had forgotten the principle "that God
in the Bible accommodates Himself to the
minds of men, and follows the laws of their
language; that other meanings besides the
literal had, at all times been admitted in certain cases, and might be admitted in many
more when circumstances required it."[65] His
theological method was thus reminiscent of
Kenrick's. In regard to inspiration, he stated
that "the fundamental position is this: THAT
INSPIRATION DOES NOT CHANGE THE
ESTABLISHED LITERARY HABITS OF
A PEOPLE OR OF A WRITER; that, con-
sequently, what is considered no departure
from truth in an ordinary book, should not
be viewed otherwise because the book is inspired." "Literary habits of a people" ac-
counted for the "substantial accuracy," though
"not exactness of detail," in the different
accounts of the Resurrection in the Synoptics
and in John.[66]

Hogan's approach to inspiration impinged
on his treatment of the Church's tradition on
the biblical narratives. He believed that Leo
XIII had left biblical scholars a certain mea-

sure of freedom in their work. He acknowledged that some Catholics might judge it "extreme" to question the story of creation or the deluge, and the date and authorship of the books of the Old and even New Testaments, but the Mosaic authorship of the Pentateuch had been "almost universally rejected by the highest Biblical authorities, and even by many of the most 'orthodox' Protestant teachers," and was "being gradually questioned among Catholic scholars." While these positions had failed to win "the approval of all," he asserted, "they are openly assumed; they are favored by some of our ablest Catholic scholars; they have been one of the salient features of the last Catholic Congress in Fribourg; and our best-known organs, in England, in France, in Germany, ventilate them freely."[67] How, then, were Catholics to reconcile these new assertions with the doctrine of inspiration?

The whole contemporary debate over inspiration, Hogan believed, resulted from two different methodologies, that of the theologians and that of the biblical scholars. He admitted that either side could go to extremes, but he thought the controversy had arisen from the fact that, while inspiration was "an article of faith, . . . what is implied thereby has never been defined, nor, perhaps, can it be defined, except by approximation." His sympathies clearly lay with the biblical scholars, for, "because of all the work that has been done on the Bible in recent times, with results which are no longer seriously questioned, theologians have to acknowledge, however reluctantly, that henceforth much less can be built on the Bible than has been done in the past." For Protestants, this might cause "dismay," he concluded, but Catholics could "contemplate it with perfect equanimity. Their faith is based, not on the Bible, but on the Church."[68] Hogan seemed almost to be turning the terminology of the prevailing theology against itself in its equation of the magisterium with tradition. For if the Church was the safeguard of truth and orthodoxy, it had little to fear from the new exegesis. He did not explicitly define what he meant by "Church," but if the lived experience of the Church were substituted for "Church," he was coming closer to what Kenrick had meant by "tradition."

Hogan was not unique among American scholars in his approach to the problem of Scripture and Tradition. His fellow Sulpician, Francis E. Gigot, S.S., also addressed the issue. In 1900, Gigot, then teaching at St. Mary's Seminary in Baltimore, had published his *General Introduction to the Study of the Holy Scriptures*. It had Corrigan's *imprimatur* and Hogan's *nihil obstat*. Like Hogan, he emphasized that Catholics had less to fear from modern criticism than Protestants, for "Catholics built their faith primarily on the teaching of a living Church, whereas Protestants rest their whole belief on the written word of God."[69] Gigot, too, saw tradition not so much as a deposit as a process of handing on the living faith.

Gigot's *General Introduction* was a relatively safe work, in which he took no definitive position on questions such as inspiration. But he intended the book as the first in a three-volume study of Scripture. In 1901, he published his *Special Introduction to the Study of the Old Testament: Part I. The Historical Books*. This also had Corrigan's *imprimatur,* but the *nihil obstat* came from James F. Driscoll, S.S., then the rector of St. Austin's College, the resi-

dence for Sulpician students in Washington,
where Gigot lived while teaching at St. Mary's
Seminary. Gigot made it obvious that his sympathies lay with those scholars who held that
the Pentateuch was not written directly by
Moses, but was a compilation from at least
four sources. [70] In regard to Jewish and Christian tradition of attributing the Pentateuch
to Moses, he added that it had no "theological
binding force," since there was "no positive
decision declaring it an article of Catholic
belief." "It is true," he continued,

> that, in their enumeration of the sacred books,
> the Fathers of Trent speak of "the five books of
> Moses, . . ." and that they speak thus without mis-
> givings as regards the authorship therein implied.
> But it is none the less true that, as clearly appears
> from the whole tenor of the discussions of the
> Council and from the very wording of their defi-
> nition, they intended to, and did actually, settle only
> the question of the *sacred* and *canonical* character
> of the books enumerated. [71]

Gigot was thus reflecting Lagrange's position
about the force of Trent's statement. But
Gigot ran into difficulty, for he was then pre-
paring the second volume of his *Special Introduction*. Because of the liberal orientation of
the first volume, his superiors in France de-

manded that he submit his manuscript to Paris for special censorship. The controversy that ensued centered precisely on the binding force of Trent's decree, especially as the biblical question became central to the Holy See's concerns.

In 1902, Leo XIII announced the establishment of the Pontifical Biblical Commission. The "first secretary" was Fulcran Vigouroux, S.S., who had earlier taught both Lagrange and Gigot. Vigouroux, as was seen, had stated that Trent was arguing for the Mosaic authorship of the Pentateuch. Late in December, 1902, Jules Joseph Lebas, S.S., the Superior General of the Sulpicians in Paris, informed Gigot that his works had been "examined with the greatest care and with perfect impartiality." The examiners, however had judged that "Fr. Gigot, in his Special Introduction . . . accepts some theories and opinions which are not in conformity with the *common teaching* of Catholics, which is all the more grave since his work is intended for seminarians." The general then enclosed a list of some of the passages which the examiners found objectionable. Gigot was instructed not to publish a second edition of his work without making

the revisions, which the examiners had noted,
and not to publish the second part of the *Special Introduction* without obtaining the approval of the general's censors in Paris.[72] The
question now became the meaning of "the
common teaching of Catholics." Gigot recognized immediately that one of the general's
censors was Vigouroux. He forwarded a copy
of Lebas' letter to Edward Dyer, S.S., the
vicar general in the United States. "The decision," he wrote, "is just what might be ex-
pected from our Superior General and his
consultors."[73]

During the next few months, Dyer sought
to work out a compromise with the advice of
his counsellors. Daniel E. Maher, Hogan's
successor as president of St. John's Seminary
in Brighton offered his own opinion on what
constituted the "common teaching" of the
Church. "We are in a period of transition,"
he wrote,

> and the ideas that the examiners of Fr. Gigot's book
> take exception to, are gaining ground amongst
> Catholic scholars, and before many years will be
> taught without opposition. I notice neither the exa-
> miners nor Fr. Lebas speak of these ideas as *erro-
> neous,* but as in *opposition* with what is *up to the pre-
> sent* the *common teaching.*[74]

Dyer and Gigot were, in the meantime, in consultation as they prepared their respective responses to Lebas' letter. Gigot even offered to omit from his second volume "every expression . . . that betrays a personal leaning towards new theories and opinions."[75]

On January 15, 1903, Gigot sent his reply to Lebas. He challenged the objections that the examiners had raised against particular passages of his book. To the charge that his position was in opposition to "the common teaching of Catholics," he replied that he was treating both old and new theories in the same manner in which Vigouroux had done in his *Manuel Biblique*. He was, however, writing in a religiously pluralistic country, where Protestant journals circulated freely, and, therefore, felt an obligation to explain old theories while discussing the new ones. Maher and Driscoll, the censors for the first volume, had, he concluded, agreed with his apologetic purpose.[76]

Dyer's letter to Lebas was a bold defense of Gigot. He labelled the report of the examiner as "grievously unjust." Though Lebas had argued that Gigot's book was dangerous to seminarians, Dyer countered that "we

think that it is necessary to prepare our
students for what they will encounter immediately after their departure from the seminary" and the biblical question was being discussed in the principal journals of the country.
Dyer then turned to consideration of the proper approach to the "common teaching" of the
Church. Gigot's two books, he noted, had
caused no controversy in the United States
and all his American superiors, including himself, had encouraged their publication. "We
believed," he continued,

> that not only was there nothing dangerous in these
> works, but rather that there was nothing contrary
> to our grand rule about the teaching in our seminar-
> ies: that it is the teaching commonly received from
> the Church which ought to be set forth. . . . But this
> rule cannot mean that this common teaching is to
> be presented as if it had almost the value of defini-
> tions of faith, as is too frequently done. It ought to
> be presented with its true theological note, other-
> wise we fall into the error which we intend to avoid,
> and we do not give the doctrine of the Church. If
> we gave opinions their true value, if we also pre-
> sented other theories, as much as possible, with their
> true theological note, would there be such disturb-
> ance of the spirit and even of faith, when it becomes
> necessary to abandon some positions held for a long
> time by the poorly instructed masses, even eccle-
> siastics, as if they were some necessary teachings
> of the Church?[77]

In the fall of 1904, Gigot joined the faculty at Dunwoodie, composed of six Sulpicians and eight diocesan priests. His case became further complicated by the decision of James Driscoll, S.S., the president of Dunwoodie, to begin publication of *The New York Review* early in 1905. A few weeks later Gigot again addressed the question of his second volume. Vigouroux, he knew, was one of the examiners of his first volume of the *Special Introduction,* and had stated that Gigot did "not teach the Catholic doctrine," particularly in regard to the "Authorship of the Pentateuch." Gigot believed that he had presented in his book the traditional view of the Mosaic authorship of the Pentateuch "with its proper theological value," namely that the Church had made no formal decision. In light of this criticism, he could not expect Vigouroux to approve publication of his second volume, and, therefore, urged Dyer to permit its publication without censorship in Paris. [78]

For the next year, Dyer sought to convince his Parisian superiors to allow Gigot's book to be censored in the United States. By January, 1906, all his efforts proved to be in vain. Driscoll, Gigot, and three other Sulpicians

announced they were withdrawing from the
Sulpicians and were remaining at Dunwoodie
as diocesan priests.[79] Relieved of the neces-
sity of obtaining special censorship in Paris,
Gigot published the second volume, his *Special
Introduction to the Study of the Old Testament,
Part II. Didactic and Prophetical Writings*.
It had the *nihil obstat* of Driscoll, as the *censor
deputatus* of the Archdiocese of New York.
Despite all the revisions Gigot had made over
the previous three years, it was still a relatively progressive work. He treated Isaiah
1-39 separately from 40-66, for example, and
mentioned the arguments of the higher critics
in favor of separate authorship. He concluded
by quoting Newman that "it does not matter
whether one or two Isaias wrote the book
which bears the prophet's name, the Church,
without settling this point, pronounces it
inspired."[80] In other words, he linked inspiration with canonicity, the Church's acceptance
of the books, rather than with authorship.

On the eve of the Modernist crisis, there
were other American exegetes attempting to
preserve a theological notion of tradition as
the lived experience of the Church. At the
Catholic University in Washington, Henry

Poels, a student of A. van Hoonacker at Louvain, was addressing the same issue. He called for a return to a careful study of the Fathers, inasmuch as they did not always adhere to a literal interpretation of the Scripture. He granted that frequently the Fathers were too free in their appeal to the spiritual sense of Scripture, but this presented little problem for Catholicism, said Poels, "since the interpretation itself was controlled by the living teaching and divine authority of the Spouse of the Holy Ghost."[81] The Church had battled Protestants for so long, he continued, that it took over their approach of adhering to "the letter" in interpreting Scripture. Far from undermining the faith, however, he suggested that "the critical study of biblical history teaches us that we must once more take up our old Catholic tradition, provided that we avoid in the interpretation of the Word of God that exaggeration of the secret and spiritual sense, which spoiled the work of some of the greatest of our ancient scholars."[82]

Unfortunately, the scholarly pleas of Gigot and Poels in the United States and of Lagrange and others elsewhere went unheeded. The Pontifical Biblical Commission, originally established by Leo XIII to promote biblical scholarship, had taken a decidedly conservative orientation under Pius X. Beginning in February, 1905, it issued a series of negative "responses" against the Scripture writers' using "implicit citations" and writing by "historical appearances."[83]

At Woodstock College, Anthony J. Maas, S.J., was delighted with the new trend. He had been given the exclusive charge of reporting on the biblical question in the *American Ecclesiastical Review.* The responses, he said, should warn against "the poison that certain readers might gather out of Dr. H.A. Poels' two articles." Patronizingly, he concluded, however, that "if Dr. Poels does not quarrel with the Biblical Commission, we will not quarrel with him."[84] But the major rebuke to the new critics was the commission's response to the Mosaic authorship of the Pentateuch.

On June 27, 1906, the commission rejected the proposal that "the arguments amassed by critics" were "of sufficient weight" to impugn the Mosaic authorship, "notwithstanding the very many evidences to the contrary contained in both Testaments, taken collectively, the persistent agreement of the Jewish people, the constant tradition of the Church, and internal arguments derived from the text itself."[85] The response embodied the theological position of the commission's first secretary, Vigouroux. In the *American Ecclesiastical Review,* an anonymous writer, probably Maas, drew the comparison between Vigouroux and the response in a review of Gigot's second volume.

The reviewer praised the new volume, but felt compelled to note that in Gigot's first volume, he "made no secret of his leanings toward the pronounced views of those critics who question the immediate authorship of some of the historical books, notably of the Pentateuch." These "leanings" had placed Gigot "in an attitude of separation from, if not contradiction to, the views of the Abbé Vigouroux, who defends the absolute Mosiac authorship of the first five books of the Bible." This was also the position taken by the Biblical Commission, and, while it was "not necessarily intended to be an infallible pronouncement of the Church," it defined "the attitude of Catholics in practical controversy." When Gigot had written his first volume, the reviewer continued, the "Catholic position had not been authoritatively defined" and, therefore, "there was no ground for criticizing the author." Once the Biblical Commission had spoken, however, it "would seem to require the revision of the chapters in Father Gigot's first volume referring to this topic, in such a manner that the student may not be biased against the evidence for the Mosaic authorship."[86] There was a certain lack of logic in the review. While the commission's response was "not necessarily . . . an infallible pronouncement," the "Catholic position" had now been "authoritatively defined."

Gigot never revised his first volume, nor did he do any further exegetical work. More tragically, in an episode containing all the elements of a very bad soap opera, Poels was forced to resign his post at the Catholic University, because he could not sign an oath that he believed "in conscience" that Moses was the author of the Pentateuch. One of his principal persecutors was Denis O'Connell, then the rector of the university. Despite his dismissal for heresy, he was retained as a consultor to the Biblical Commission until his death in 1946.[87]

The biblical exegetes at the beginning of

the century had much in common with Kenrick of an earlier era. Lagrange, Hogan, and Poels all explicitly derived their notion of tradition as the lived experience of the Church from a study of the Fathers, rather than the scholastics. In the later twentieth century, their notion of tradition became lost in the American Catholic mind, for they had tried to express it in the midst of the crisis of Modernism. Just as the Americanists had run afoul of the conservative interpretation of the papal magisterium on Church-State relations, the biblicists, in part at least, faced the opposition of the conservative interpretation of "tradition" of the Tridentine decree.

Pius X re-enforced the concept of tradition as a deposit and emphatically rejected any notion of it as a lived experience. In *Pascendi Dominici Gregis,* he stated that the Modernists premised their religious belief on individual experience, which, "extended and applied to tradition, as hitherto understood by the Church . . . destroys it. By the modernists tradition is understood as a communication to others, through preaching, by means of the intellectual formula, of an original experience." "For the modernists," he continued, "to live is a proof of truth, since for them life and truth are one and the same thing." From such a principle, he concluded, the Modernists inferred "that all existing religions are equally true, for otherwise they would not live."[88] This, of course, was a misrepresentation of tradition as experience in the sense in which Catholic theologians like Kenrick, Hogan, Gigot or Poels would have used it. Later theologians would further modify the concept of tradition to make it a yet more immutable deposit.

III. Tradition in the Twentieth Century

Louis Billot, S.J., professor of dogmatic theology at the Gregorian University, was so characteristic of the new theological approach as to be a caricature. In 1904, he published the first edition of his *De sacra Traditione contra novam haeresim evolutionismi.* Contending with Alfred Loisy's assertion that "the concepts which the Church presents as revealed dogmas are not truths fallen from heaven," Billot confidently declared that concepts, though human in origin, once put to-

gether to formulate doctrines proposed to
faith on the authority of God Who reveals, do
in fact come down from heaven. In case any-
one missed Billot's approach to tradition, he
changed the title of his work in the second and
subsequent editions to: *De immutabilitate tra-
ditionis contra modernam haeresim evolutionismi.* [89] Unfortunately, Billot was neither
an insignificant figure nor an aberration. In
1911, he was named a cardinal, but in 1927,
was forced to resign because of his support
of *Action Française.* He died in 1931, but the
legacy of his theology of "immutable tradition" lived on. As late as the 1950s, his approach to the theology of tradition was still
the standard fare at the Jesuits' Woodstock
College. [90]

The condemnation of Modernism argu-
ably had more of an impact on the United
States than elsewhere, for American Catholic
intellectual life was then in its infancy, and,
even then, was largely derivative from
Europe. The new theological orientation was
equally European in origin, but with a distinc-
tively different cast of mind. Roman manuals
of theology replaced the historically based
theology of a Hogan or a Gigot. [91] On the

biblical question, Maas continued to be the
sole reporter in the *American Ecclesiastical
Review,* until he was named provincial superior of the Maryland-New York Province in
1912. His place in the *Review* was taken by
his successor as professor of Scripture at
Woodstock, Walter Drum. Committed to a
war against Modernism, Drum ceased writing
for the *Review,* when the editor refused to
publish one of Drum's articles calling for
works of C.C. Martindale, S.J., to be placed
on the Index of Forbidden Books. [92]

Neo-Thomism held full sway, especially
after World War I, [93] but it was the form of
Thomism of which Billot and his imitators
were so exemplary. All truth was reduced to
syllogisms, and, as often as not, dogmatic
theology consisted in the mere analysis of
words. Research was restricted to a repetition
of the past. In 1938, George Bull, S.J., dean
of the Graduate School at Fordham University, said it well when he spoke of the purpose
of graduate education. It was for the secular
graduate school "to add to the sum of human
knowledge." But the purpose of the Catholic
graduate school was different, for the Church
was in full possession of the truth. "The

Catholic mind," he continued, had a "totality of view," which was

> the simple assumption that wisdom has been achieved by man, and that the humane use of the mind, the function proper to him as man, is contemplation and not research . . . . In sum, then, research cannot be the primary object of a Catholic graduate school, because it is at war with the whole Catholic life of the mind. [94]

Nothing could have been more of an affirmation of immutable tradition. The interpretation of a particular school was becoming confused with doctrine itself. Such was the fate of the Church-State question in American Catholic thought.

In 1922, John A. Ryan of the Catholic University addressed the issue in *The State and the Church,* a book edited with Moorhouse F.X. Millar, S.J. "The State should officially recognize the Catholic religion as the religion of the Commonwealth," he declared, "for error has not the same rights as truth." Such an abstract formulation was far removed from O'Connell's statement, but it was the one used right through the first session of Vatican II. Ryan recognized, however, that these principles "have full application only to the com-

pletely Catholic state" – a situation that would
not be realized in the United States for "some
five thousand years hence," if ever. Unpopular
though this position might be among Protestants, Ryan declared that "we cannot yield up
the principles of eternal and unchangeable
truth in order to avoid the enmity of . . .
unreasonable persons."[95] For Ryan at this
stage, the teaching of the "Syllabus of Errors"
now participated in the "immutability of tradition" so dear to Billot. In fairness to Ryan,
however, he later nuanced his position and
came closer to Dupanloup's original use of
"thesis" and "hypothesis."[96]

Biblical studies shared in this theological
mind set. In 1937, the Catholic Biblical Association was founded. In 1943, its journal, *The
Catholic Biblical Quarterly,* published three
articles commemorating the fiftieth anniver-
sary of *Providentissimus Deus.* Each of them
considered the "doctrine" of inspiration to
have been permanently settled in the encyclical. They all accepted "tradition" as something
static and unchanging and statements of the
Biblical Commission as unconditioned by historical circumstances.[97] The articles could
have well been written at the beginning of the

century in the height of the reaction against Modernism. Neither of them gave any indication that what they were presenting was not the immutable truth of tradition, nor did they give any indication of the new intellectual winds beginning to blow in Rome.

Piux XII had prepared his own commemoration of Leo XIII's encyclical. Americans were ill prepared to read in *Divino Afflante Spiritu* that the Scripture writers had used the literary forms of their own languages to express their thoughts and that, therefore, Catholic exegetes should use historical criticism in discovering the intention of the authors. The "tradition" of the Church had not been nearly as immutable as the American writers in the CBQ had thought. It would take the American Church more than two decades to grapple with the apparently new thought, whose acceptance would come only after struggle.

There were other currents of thought beginning to flow into Catholic theology and its understanding of tradition. In post-war France, theologians re-examined the Fathers of the Church, who had been so influential on Kenrick and on the Catholic exegetes of the early twentieth-century. The "New Theology" that emerged reshaped the Thomism, which had become identified with doctrine.[98] Closer to home, John Courtney Murray, S.J., began addressing the neuralgic problem of the Catholic teaching on Church-State relations. Wishing to avoid the pitfalls of Ryan a generation earlier, Murray argued that no historically conditioned relationship between Church and State could in fact be a "thesis" or doctrine. He met with opposition from Monsignor Joseph C. Fenton, professor of theology at the Catholic University, who argued that Murray's position was condemned in the "infallible" doctrine of *Longinqua Oceani*. To minimize that teaching simply to gain acceptance in the United States made Murray subject to the condemnation contained in the equally infallible *Testem Benevolentiae*. These apostolic letters contained for Fenton and his associates defined doctrine.[99]

The period 1950 to 1963 represented a virtual replay of the controversies over Americanism and the biblical question at the turn of the century. Murray and the biblical scholars both faced opposition from the same sources, Fenton and other contributors to the

American Ecclesiastical Review and later Cardinal Alfredo Ottaviani and Archbishop Egidio Vagnozzi, the apostolic delegate to the American hierarchy. The issues were also the same – the nature of ordinary teaching and the binding force of papal pronouncements. The opponents to Murray and the biblical scholars argued not only that tradition was a static deposit to be interpreted primarily by the papal magisterium, but also that the expressions of the magisterium were to be interpreted literally.

In 1950, Pius XII seemed to re-enforce their position in *Humani Generis*. The role of the theologian, said Pius, was to return to "the sources of revelation: for to them belongs the task of pointing out how the teachings of the living Magisterium are found, whether explicitly or implicitly, in Scripture and divine tradition."[100] Here seemed to be a clear papal affirmation of two separate sources of revelation. The pope, however, avoided stating that papal interpretations of tradition in encyclicals were infallible.[101] But in the minds of Fenton and Ottaviani, encyclicals and even apostolic letters did enjoy infallibility and were, therefore, irreversible. Though the en-

cyclical was aimed primarily at the "new theologians,"[102] the repercussions were felt in
other areas of theological research.

In March, 1953, Ottaviani, recently named
a cardinal, gave an address at the Lateran
Seminary. Where Catholics were in the majority, he said, there should be a union of
Church and State; where Catholics were in
the minority, the Church should have freedom. He freely acknowledged that this was
"a truly embarrassing double standard," for
"two weights and two measures are to be applied: one for truth, the other for error."
Without mentioning Murray's name, he rejected the "erroneous theories . . . being set
forth also in America." He did, however, explicitly cite one of Fenton's articles in the
American Ecclesiastical Review, and added
the comment that it was "sad to note" how
a certain "writer takes exception to the
teaching set forth in the Manuals of Public
Ecclesiastical Law, without taking into account the fact that this teaching is for the
most part based on the doctrine set forth in
Pontifical documents."[103] Quite clearly Ottaviani considered that "doctrine" to be immua-
table. His position that error has no rights

was almost a caricature of the school of Thomism, which had dominated the Roman schools since the late nineteenth century.

Ottaviani's speech in its entirety was never published. Fenton later published a version, but omitted all references to the United States and his own article. [104] Nevertheless, the opposition was building up against Murray and, in the summer of 1955, he received word from his superiors in Rome that he should not publish on the Church-State question in view of the increasing hostility of the Holy Office and his enemies in the United States. [105] For the moment, the entrenched theological notion of the immutable binding force of papal statements was enforced.

With Murray then silent, Fenton gradually turned his attention to biblical scholars. In the pages of the *American Ecclesiastical Review,* he and Francis Connell, C.Ss.R., began a series of attacks on the new exegesis which had developed from *Divino Afflante Spiritu.* For the biblical question, as for that of Church-State relations, the issue was one of the immutable tradition interpreted in papal documents and statements of the Biblical Commission. In his attack on biblical scholarship, Fenton received the assistance in 1958 of the new apostolic delegate, Archbishop Vagnozzi. In 1961, the Catholic Biblical Association counter-attacked with a resolution condemning certain articles that had appeared in the *American Ecclesiastical Review.* One of the articles cited was the text of an address Vagnozzi had given at Marquette University, in which he challenged the orthodoxy of Biblical exegetes. The resolution with its explicit mention of the *Review,* however, was never published. Vagnozzi used his influence on Archbishop Patrick O'Boyle of Washington not to give his *imprimatur* for the publication. [106]

The biblical controversy, too, had its victim. At the Catholic University, Edward Siegman, C.Pp.S., had been teaching Scripture since 1951 and had been the editor of the *Catholic Biblical Quarterly* from 1951 to 1958. In the Spring of 1962, he was on sick leave from the university and was informed that the university had hired a replacement for him. He had been a particular target of Fenton and Vagnozzi and knew that he was dismissed for his liberal exegesis. [107]

Despite the centrality of the theological

notion of tradition in the discussions on both Church-State relations and the biblical question, it was never explicitly treated. As the American Church prepared for the opening of Vatican II, its scholars were on the defensive. Fenton had been invited to the council as a *peritus* for Ottaviani. Murray remained at home at Woodstock College, "disinvited," to use his term, at the express command of Ottaviani.[108] During the summer of 1962, the first schema on "the sources of revelation," drafted by Ottaviani, was circulated. It caused great consternation among the members of the Catholic Biblical Association at their annual meeting.[109] John L. Murphy delivered a paper pointing out that the Council of Trent had, in fact, not stated that there were two sources. Ironically, Murphy had written one of the articles in the *American Ecclesiastical Review,* which the Catholic Biblical Association had found offensive.[110] But this discussion was in the academic arena and did not directly influence the bishops, many of whom accepted the theological opinion expressed in the Roman manuals as the official doctrine of the Church.

During the first session of the council, none

of the American bishops who spoke on the proposed schema specifically addressed the question of Tradition. Most of the council fathers, however, had severe reservations with the schema, but, unfortunately, they failed to gain the necessary two thirds majority to reject the schema. John XXIII, however, intervened and ordered the schema to be withdrawn and submitted to a mixed commission composed of members of the Theological Commission and the Secretariat for Promoting Christian Unity.[111] The first session was a significant theological turning point and a learning experience for the American bishops. The Secretariat had gained equal status with the Theological Commission in producing schemata. Among these new documents was the Constitution on Ecumenism, one chapter of which dealt with the question of religious liberty. At the end of the session, Cardinal Francis Spellman of New York gained the appointment of John Courtney Murray as a *peritus*.

It took three years for the council to work out satisfactory statements on both religious liberty and the relationship between Scripture and Tradition. The story of the American contribution to what became the "Declaration on Religious Liberty" has been told elsewhere.[112] Suffice it to say here that such a declaration would have been impossible without a new theology of tradition. In addition to the opposition of Ottaviani and other representatives of the Roman schools, however, Murray and Pietro Pavan's juridical approach to religious liberty did not satisfy those theologians who wished to see the subject grounded in an adequate theology of the person. Such a theology would come from the constitution on revelation, and it is provocative to note that Pierre Benoit, O.P., the exegete and successor to Lagrange at the École Biblique, assisted in drafting the final declaration.

The constitution on revelation, on which the bishops voted in 1965, was totally different from the one on "the sources of revelation." It had been principally shaped by the concerns for the relation between Scripture and Tradition and for the historicity and inerrancy of the Scripture in light of historical criticism. *Dei Verbum* stated that "Sacred tradition and sacred Scripture make up a single sacred deposit of the Word of God, which is entrusted to the Church." It belonged to the "living teaching office of the Church alone," however, to give "an authentic interpretation of the Word of God, whether in its written form or in the form of Tradition."[113] Tradition was given a more dynamic meaning than it had had in the Roman theology since Vatican I. As Joseph Ratzinger noted, "it is not difficult . . . to recognize the pen of Y. Congar in the text and to see behind it the influence of the Catholic Tübingen school of the nineteenth century with, in particular, its dynamic and organic idea of tradition."[114] Had he known it, the future cardinal could also have added the name of Francis Kenrick. The new theology of tradition was close to the old theology of the American Church.

NOTES

1. See Joseph Ratzinger, "Dogmatic Constitution on Divine Revelation: Origin and Background," in Herbert Vorgrimler (ed.), *Commentary on the Documents of Vatican II* (New York: Herder and Herder, 1969), III, 156-157.

2. *Ibid.,* 159-160.

3. Thomas O. Hanley, S.J. (ed.), *The John Carroll Papers* (3 vols.; University of Notre Dame Press, 1976), I, 111.

4. *Ibid.,* 137-138.

5. James Hennesey, S.J., "An Eighteenth Century Bishop: John Carroll of Baltimore," *Archivum Historiae Pontificiae,* 16 (1978), 171-204.

6. Hugh J. Nolan (ed.), *The Pastoral Letters of the American Hierarchy, 1792-1970* (Huntington, Ind.: Our Sunday Visitor, 1970), p. 51.

7. *Ibid.,* 52.

8. Francis Patrick Kenrick, *Theologia Dogmatica* (4 vols.; 2nd ed.; Baltimore: John Murphy & Co., 1858), I, 282-283.

9. *Ibid.,* 288.

10. *Ibid.,* 289.

11. *Ibid.,* 300-301.

12. *Ibid.,* 301.

13. *Ibid.,* 302.

14. *Ibid.,* 302.

15. *Ibid.*, 306.

16. *Ibid.*, 365-370.

17. *Ibid.*, 227-228.

18. Francis Patrick Kenrick, *The Pentateuch* (Baltimore: Kelly, Hedian & Piet, 1860), pp. 17-18.

19. *Ibid.*, 18-19.

20. Gerald A. McCool, S.J., *Catholic Theology in the Nineteenth Century: The Quest for a Unitary Method* (New York: The Seabury Press, 1977), pp. 129-140.

21. Quoted in Roger Aubert, *Le pontificat de Pie IX* (1846-1878), vol. 21 of *Histoire de l'eglise depuis les origines jusqu'à nos jours* (Paris: Bloud & Gay, 1952), p. 354.

22. DS, 3011.

23. DS, 3019.

24. DS, 1501.

25. DS, 3006.

26. Yves M.-J. Congar, O.P., *Traditions and Tradition: An Historical and a Theological Essay EHP1.* (New York: The MacMillan Company, 1967), p. 198. See also Walter J. Burghardt, S.J., "The Catholic Concept of Tradition in the Light of Modern Theological Thought," *Proceedings of the Sixth Annual Convention of the Catholic Theological Society of America* (1951), pp. 48-49.

27. McCool, p. 233.

28. *Ibid.*

29. For Maryland, see Gerald P. Fogarty, S.J., "Property and Religious Liberty in Colonial Maryland Catholic Thought," *Catholic Historical Review,* 72 (1986), 573-600.

30. Nolan, *Pastoral Letters of the American Hierarchy,* pp. 66-67.

31. Gregory XVI, *Mirari Vos,* in Colman J. Barry, O.S.B., *Readings in Church History* (3 vols.; Paramus, N.J.: Newman Press, 1965), III, 37-44, especially, pp. 41, 43.

32. Henri Haag, *Les Origines du Catholicisme Libéral en Belgique: 1789-1839* (Louvain: Nauwelaerts, 1950), pp. 183, 191-192, cited in Thomas J. Shelley, "Mutual Independence: Church and State in Belgium: 1825-1846," unpublished seminar paper, The Catholic University of America, April, 1985, pp. 20-21.

33. DS, 2955.

34. DS, 2977.

35. Quoted in James Hennesey, S.J., "The Baltimore Council of 1866: An American Syllabus," *Records of the American Catholic Historical Society,* 76 (1965), 162.

36. Roger Aubert, "Monseigneur Dupanloup et le Syllabus," *Revue d'histoire ecclésiastique,* 51 (1956), 117-120. See also Marvin R. O'Connell, "Ultramontanism and Dupanloup: The Compromise of 1865," *Church History,* 53 (1984), 215.

37. Quoted in John Lancaster Spalding, *The Life of the Most Rev. M.J. Spalding* (New York, 1873), pp. 272-273, in James Hennesey, S.J., "The Baltimore Council of 1866: An American Syllabus" p. 164.

38. Leo XIII, *Longinqua Oceani,* in John Tracy Ellis (ed.), *Documents of American Catholic History* (Chicago: Henry Regnery Company, 1967), p. 507.

39. Gerald P. Fogarty, S.J., *The Vatican and the Americanist Crisis: Denis J. O'Connell, American Agent in Rome: 1885-1903* (Rome: Università Gregoriana Editrice, 1974), pp. 266.

40. *La Vérité,* Mar. 19, 1898.

41. McAvoy, *Great Crisis,* pp. 189-198.

42. Archives of the Archdiocese of St. Paul, O'Connell to Ireland, Rome, July 12, 1898.

43. Francesco Turvasi, *Giovanni Genocchi e la Controversia Modernista* (Rome: Edizioni di storia e letteratura, 1974), p. 98.

44. *Père Lagrange: Personal Reflections and Memoirs,* translated by Rev. Henry Wansbrough (New York: Paulist Press, 1985), pp. 62-63, 67-68.

45. Leo XIII, *Testem Benevolentiae,* in: John Tracy Ellis (ed.), *Documents of American Catholic History* (2 vols.; Chicago: Henry Regnery Co., 1967), II, 539.

46. *Ibid.,* 541-542.

47. *Ibid.,* 543.

48. Fogarty, *The Vatican and the American Hierarchy From 1870 to 1965* (Stuttgart: Anton Hiersemann Verlag, 1982; paperback: Wilmington, Del.: Michael Glazier, 1985), pp. 180-183.

49. *Père Lagrange,* pp. 68-69.

50. *Ibid.,* 70.

51. *Ibid.,* 74-75.

52. Pierre Benoit, O.P., *Aspects of Biblical Inspiration,* translated by J. Murphy-O'Connor, O.P., and S.K. Ashe, O.P. (Chicago: The Priory Press, 1965), pp. 55-64.

53. James Tunstead Burtchaell, C.S.C., *Catholic Theories of Biblical Inspiration since 1810: A Review and Critique* (Cambridge, 1969), 98-99.

54. DS, 3006.

55. Leo XIII, *Providentissimus Deus,* in: *Rome and the Study of Scripture* (St. Meinrad's, Ind. 1962), p. 22.

56. *Ibid.,* 23.

57. *Ibid.,* 24.

58. *Ibid.*

59. Turvasi, *Genocchi,* p. 93.

60. F. Vigouroux, *Les livres saints et la critique ration-aliste: histoire et réfutation des objections des incré-dules contre les saintes écritures* (5 vols.: Paris: A. Roger & F. Chernoviz, 1890), I, 9-10.

61. Quoted in Joseph Bruneau, S.S., "A Page of Con-temporary History," *American Ecclesiastical Review,* 14 (1896), 252.

62. M.-J. Lagrange, "Miscellaneous: On the Penta-teuch," *The Catholic University Bulletin,* 4 (1898), 119-120.

63. *Ibid.,* 120.

64. John B. Hogan, *Clerical Studies* (Boston: Marlier, Callahan & Co., 1898), pp. 427-428.

65. *Ibid.,* 471-472.,

66. *Ibid.,* 474.

67. *Ibid.,* 476-477.

68. *Ibid.,* 480-481.

69. Francis E. Gigot, S.S., *General Introduction to the Study of the Holy Scriptures* (New York: Benzinger Brothers, 1900), p. 517.

70. Francis E. Gigot, S.S., *Special Introduction to the Study of the Old Testament: Part 1. The Historical Books* (New York: Benzinger Brothers, 1901), 85-141. For a detailed analysis of this work, see Bernard Joseph Noone, "A Critical Analysis of the American Catholic Response to Higher Criticism as Reflected in Selected Catholic Periodicals: 1870 to 1908," unpublished Ph.D. dissertation, Drew Univer-sity, 1976, pp. 331-376.

71. Gigot, *Special Introduction,* I, 32.

72. Sulpician Archives, Baltimore (hereafter SAB), Lebas to Gigot, Paris, Dec. 24, 1902 (copy).

73. SAB, Gigot to Dyer, Washington, Jan. 4, 1903.

74. SAB, Maher to Dyer, Brighton, Jan. 11, 1903.

75. SAB, Gigot to Dyer, Baltimore, Jan. 14, 1903.

76. SAB, Gigot to Lebas, Washington, Jan. 15, 1903 (copy).

77. SAB, Dyer to Lebas, Baltimore, Jan. 18, 1903 (copy). Dyer noted on the top of the letter that he had sent the original on Jan. 21, 1903.

78. SAB, Gigot to Dyer, Dunwoodie, Feb. 13, 1905.

79. E.R. Dyer, S.S., *Letters on the New York Seminary Secession* (Baltimore, 1906), pp. 57-67. Originally published in English and French, this was circulated among Sulpicians in the United States and France, the former Sulpicians at Dunwoodie, and the apostolic delegate.

80. Francis E. Gigot, *Special Introduction to the Study of the Old Testament, Part II. Didactic Books and Prophetical Writings* (New York: Benzinger Brothers, 1906), 249-265.

81. Henry Poels, "History and Inspiration. I. The Fathers of the Church," *The Catholic University Bulletin,* 11 (Apr., 1905), 189.

82. *Ibid.,* 190.

83. DS, 3372-3373, in *Rome and the Study of Scripture,* p. 117-118.

84. Anthony J. Maas, "Ecclesiastical Library Table: Recent Bible Study," *American Ecclesiastical Review,* 32 (June, 1905), 654.

85. DS, 3394, in *Rome and the Study of Scripture,* p. 118.

86. Unsigned, "Criticisms and Notes," *American Ecclesiastical Review,* 35 (Oct., 1906), 435-436.

87. Henry A. Poels, "A Vindication of My Honor," edited with an introduction by Frans Neirynck in *Annua Nuntia Lovaniensia,* 225 (1982). A copy of this lengthy account is in the Archives of the Archdiocese of Baltimore and in the Archives of the Catholic University of America. For a popular article on the Poels case, see Gerald P. Fogarty, S.J., "Dissent at the Catholic University: The Case of Henry Poels," *America,* 156 (Oct. 11, 1986), 180-184.

88. Pius X, *Pascendi Dominici Gregis* in Claudia Carlen, I.H.M., *The Papal Encyclicals: 1903-1939* (Raleigh: A Consortium Book, 1981), p. 77. This passage is not given in DS; see Congar, p. 207.

89. Gabriel Daly, O.S.A., *Transcendence and Immanence: A Study in Catholic Modernism and Integralism* (Oxford: The Clarendon Press, 1980), p. 176.

90. Burghardt, p. 61.

91. Michael V. Gannon, "Before and After Modernism: The Intellectual Isolation of the American Priest," in John Tracy Ellis (ed.), *The Catholic Priest in the United States: Historical Investigations* (Collegeville, Minn.: Saint John's University Press, 1971), pp. 351-354.

92. Archives of Woodstock College, II, A.10.7a (4), Heuser to Drum, Overbrook, Pa., Oct. 7, 1920.

93. For the dominance of Thomism, see William M. Halsey, *The Survival of American Innocence: Catholicism in an Era of Disillusionment* (Notre Dame, Ind.: University of Notre Dame Press, 1980), pp. 138-168.

94. Quoted in Gannon, pp. 358-359.

95. Quoted in Francis L. Broderick, *Right Reverend New Dealer: John A. Ryan* (New York: The Macmillan Company, 1963), pp. 119-120.

96. *Ibid.,* 176-177.

97. Anthony J. Cotter, S.J., "The Antecedents of the Encyclical *Providentissimus Deus,"* CBQ, 5 (1943), 117-124; Richard T. Murphy, O.P., "The Teachings of the Encyclical *Providentissimus Deus," ibid.,* 125-140; Stephen J. Hartdegan, O.F.M., "The Influence of the Encyclical *Providentissimus Deus* on the Subsequent Study of Scripture," *ibid.,* 141-159.

98. McCool, pp. 257-259.

99. Donald E. Pelotte, S.S.S., *John Courtney Murray: Theologian in Conflict* (New York: The Paulist Press, 1975), pp. 154-173.

100. DS, 3886.

101. DS, 3885.

102. McCool, pp. 259-260.

103. Quoted in Fogarty, *Vatican and the American Hierarchy,* pp. 371-372.

104. *Ibid.,* 372-375.

105. Pelotte, pp. 52-53.

106. *Catholic Biblical Quarterly,* 23 (1961), 470. Copies of the original resolution with references to the offending articles are in the archives of the Catholic Biblical Association at the Catholic University.

107. Archives of the Congregation of the Most Precious Blood, Carthagena, Ohio, Siegman memorandum.

108. Pelotte, p. 77.

109. Raymond E. Brown, S.S., to author, New York, Feb. 3, 1987.

110. *Catholic Biblical Quarterly,* 24 (1962), 421. Murphy's paper was not published in the CBQ, but he had written an earlier article on the topic; see John L. Murphy, "Unwritten Traditions at Trent," *American Ecclesiastical Review,* 146 (1962), 233-263.

111. Ratzinger, p. 161.

112. Pelotte, pp. 77-100.

113. *Dei Verbum,* no. 2, in: Austin Flannery, O.P. (ed.), *Vatican Council II: the Conciliar and Post Conciliar Documents* (Collegeville, Minn.: The Liturgical Press, 1975), pp. 750-751.

114. Ratzinger, p. 184.

The Pere Marquette Theology Lectures

1969: "The Authority for Authority,"
by Quentin Quesnell
Professor of Theology
Marquette University

1970: "Mystery and Truth,"
by John Macquarrie
Professor of Theology
Union Theological Seminary, New York

1971: "Doctrinal Pluralism,"
by Bernard Lonergan, S.J.
Professor of Theology
Regis College, Ontario

1972: "Infallibility,"
by George A. Lindbeck
Professor of Theology
Yale University

1973: "Ambiguity in Moral Choice,"
by Richard A. McCormick, S.J.
Professor of Moral Theology
Bellarmine School of Theology

1974: "Church Membership as a Catholic
and Ecumenical Problem,"
by Avery Dulles, S.J.
Professor of Theology
Woodstock College

1975: "The Contributions of Theology to
Medical Ethics,"
by James Gustafson
University Professor of Theological Ethics
University of Chicago

1976: "Religious Values in an Age of Violence,"
by Rabbi Marc Tanenbaum
Director of National Interreligious Affairs
American Jewish Committee, New York City

1977: "Truth Beyond Relativism: Karl Mannheim's Sociology of Knowledge,"
by Gregory Baum
Professor of Theology and Religious Studies
St. Michael's College

1978: "A Theology of 'Uncreated Energies' "
by George A. Maloney, S.J.
Professor of Theology
John XXIII Center For Eastern Christian Studies
Fordham University

1980: "Method in Theology: An Organon For Our Time,"
by Frederick E. Crowe, S.J.
Research Professor in Theology
Regis College, Toronto

1981: "Catholics in the Promised Land of the Saints,"
by James Hennesey, S.J.
Professor of the History of Christianity
Boston College

1982: "Whose Experience Counts in Theological Reflection?"
by Monika Hellwig
Professor of Theology
Georgetown University

1983: "The Theology and Setting of Discipleship in the Gospel of Mark,"
by John R. Donahue, S.J.
Professor of Theology
Jesuit School of Theology, Berkeley

1984: "Should War be Eliminated? Philosophical and Theological Investigations,"
by Stanley Hauerwas
Professor of Theology
Notre Dame University

1985   "From Vision to Legislation:
From the Council to a Code of Laws,"
by Ladislas M. Orsy, S.J.
Professor of Canon Law
Catholic University of America
Washington, D.C.

1986   "Revelation and Violence:
A Study in Contextualization,"
by Walter Brueggemann
Professor of Old Testament
Eden Theological Seminary
St. Louis, Missouri

1987   "Novo Et Vetera: The Theology of Tradition
in American Catholicism,"
by Gerald Fogarty
Professor of Religious Studies
University of Virginia

Uniform format, cover and binding.

Copies of this Lecture and the others in the
series are obtainable from:

Marquette University Press
Marquette University
Milwaukee, Wisconsin 53233, U.S.A.